Working with Clay

An introduction to clay molding and sculpting

By

Léonce Philibert

Working with Clay

Copyright © 2017

ISBN: 9781520260242

Warning and Disclaimer

Every effort has been made to make this book as accurate as possible. However, no warranty or fitness is implied. The information provided is on an "as-is" basis. The author and the publisher shall have no liability or responsibility to any person or entity with respect to any loss or damages that arise from the information in this book.

Publisher contact

Skinny Bottle Publishing

books@skinnybottle.com

Introduction

When it comes to creating a work of art, there is nothing quite so visceral as being able to create something with your bare hands. Sculpting clay is a very rewarding craft because it does not require a range of specialized tools or any really complicated techniques. You can set your own pace. In addition, there is a lot of scope for experimentation once you have learned the basics.

In this book, we will go through the basic tools and techniques to get you started. We will look at the whole process from start to finish – you will learn how to prepare the clay, how to form it into the shape you want – we look at doing this by hand or by wheel – how to decorate it and how to fire it.

You will learn about the tools that you absolutely have to have, and ones that are just nice to have.

At the end of this book, you will be able to start making your own clay masterpieces and, once you get started, you will be hooked – there is nothing nicer than being able to look at a piece of pottery or sculpture and know that you created it from scratch, on your own.

Clay is a medium that is extremely versatile and very forgiving – even your mistakes can be recycled in one form or another so there is little waste.

Let's get stuck in, shall we?

Materials

To start off with, all you really need is clay. As you progress, you can look at additives to color the clay or glazes to create a different effect when firing the clay.

What is Clay?

Clay is found all over the world and is basically a fine-grained material. Its primary components are Alumina and Silica. Clay forms naturally from the erosion of granite and other rocks.

There are two types of clays that occur naturally:

Primary/ Residual Clays: This type of clay is found in situ where it originally formed. It is rarer than the secondary clays. Kaolin and Bentonite.

Sedimentary/ Secondary Clays: These are a lot more common and have undergone further weathering before being moved from where they were formed by the elements.

Is Natural or Prepared Clay Better?

This is largely a matter of personal preference and accessibility. If for example, you have a natural clay deposit in your back yard, you are more likely to consider using that clay. That said, there are a number of times when you need to mix different types of clay together in order to get the qualities that you want. Kaolin clay, for example, generally needs to be mixed with another form of clay because it is non-elastic on its own and so difficult to work.

The Six Main Clay Types

These are the types of clay that you are most likely to be working with:

Kaolin Clay also called China clay: this is very fine and white but it is hard to work with because it is not elastic in nature. It is generally used mixed with other clays or into glazes.

Bentonite Clay: This is often used to improve the elasticity of clay mixes and can be used in a concentration of about 2% in glazes to improve the suspension. It is important that you mix it thoroughly with the other ingredients before adding water or it will not become properly incorporated.

Stoneware Clay: This is not usually naturally occurring and is generally a mixture of minerals and other clays. When fired it becomes a light buff or white color. In this case, it is the minerals added that make the most difference to the finished product.

Ball Clay: This is a really fine clay and has great elastic properties. It is, however, too elastic to use on its own and so is used as a component in a mix. When fired it becomes white or off-white and it is commonly used when making stoneware and porcelain.

Fire Clay: This clay can withstand very high temperatures. It can be used as is and will become buff in color when fired.

Red Surface Clay: This clay is the most common of the natural clays and has a lot of iron in it. This is where it gets its red color from.

Choosing and Storing Your Clay

It is better to buy a little more than you think you might need, just to ensure that you do not run out at a crucial moment. When choosing the clay, consider what the final look that you want to achieve is and choose accordingly. If necessary, ask the supplier for advice on the best type of clay for your needs.

When not in used, clay should be kept in an airtight bag in a cool and dark place. If exposed to air or too much heat, it will dry out and become unworkable.

If you are not using the clay straight away, do check it occasionally to see whether or not it is drying out. If it is, wet an old towel, wrap the clay with it and then seal back in the bag for a few days. If it is really dry, make a few holes in the bag and put into a bucket of water for about 4-6 hours. Allow the water to drain and reseal.

If these methods do not work, cut the clay up into small bits, leave to dry out and then process again as if from scratch.

Other Additives

As you progress, you will want to add in other elements so that your work is more interesting.

Additives for Texture:

Feldspar: Creates a beautiful effect when used in conjunction with stoneware – kneaded into the clay, it creates beautiful explosions on the surface of the finished product.

Dry Porcelain: Crush into course bits and knead into the clay to produce lumps of texture in the finished product.

Grog: This is clay that has already been fired. Grind into a powder and knead in to improve the strength and texture of the finished piece.

Grit: This is especially useful when creating textures in sculptures. Some of the pieces might remain whole and lend a coarse finish.

Molochite – Coarse: Comes in large pieces and is used to add texture to sculptures.

Molochite – Fine: Has been powdered and is used instead of grog when the whiteness of the mixture needs to be maintained.

Basic Tools

In this chapter, we will go through the tools that you may find helpful to use. If you do not have all of these, it is not the end of the world – most of the time you can improvise as necessary.

A Knife: you can choose to get a specialized potter's knife or, if you do not want to go to that expense, you can use a plain old craft knife. As long as the blade is sharp, both will work equally well.

Rasp Blades: This is something that you really do need to consider getting – they help to reduce the bulk on clay surfaces, create more even surfaces and even texture. You can also use a fine-toothed cheese grater as a substitute.

Rubber Kidneys: You should get at least one – these help to shape, compact and smooth the clay surface.

A Potter's Needle: This tool is used to mark levels, let out excess air or for making holes. A hat pin does a comparable job at a fraction of the cost.

Hole Cutter: Again here, you can improvise quite nicely – the way these work is that you push them into the clay and then rotate them until you have a suitably sized hole. You can replicate this effect by using a ball point pen, nib removed or a pipe that has had the rough edges sanded down.

Paint Scraper: This is great for lifting little leftover scraps of clay from your work surfaces.

Loop or Ribbon Tools: These are not strictly necessary but can come in handy when you need to trim edges or hollow something out.

A Turntable: Again, not an essential tool to acquire but one that definitely makes your life easier by allowing for ease of movement of the project when trimming, etc. Alternatively, use a lazy Susan or make your own lazy Susan by taking two pie plates, one a little smaller than the other and a bag of marbles. Empty the marbles into the bigger pie plate and then put the smaller pie plate on top of this one. This creates a quick and easy lazy Susan.

Modeling Tools: You can get these at most craft stores but do not go too overboard when it comes to how many you do buy. You only need a few, not necessarily a whole set.

Wooden Spoons and Spatulas: These come in handy when it comes smoothing the clay or beating out the air. They can also be useful when it comes to creating textures. It should be noted, however, that they cannot be put back into the kitchen for general use again.

Calipers: It can be tough to get the right measurements, especially working with curved surfaces in wet clay. Calipers can help to ensure lids made will fit and that the piece is properly proportioned.

Brushes: You are going to need a few brushes – large and small to help apply glazes and luster. It is also a good idea to hang onto an old, soft toothbrush to spatter glaze onto the item or to score lines into it. A soft-headed, big fluffy brush, like a shaving brush, is ideal to clear off loose bits of clay when you are busy working.

Sponges: Have a few sponges on hand to mop up excess water from the surface of the item. Have a range of sponges in shapes and sizes that you feel you might need.

Slip Trailers: These are very useful, especially when you are doing fine work. Alternatively, a medicine dropper or any bottle with a fine nozzle can be used.

Tools for Specific Purposes

There is a range of tools designed for use by potters but they can work out quite expensive. Fortunately, you can improvise a lot of the tools necessary. In this section, we will go through tools to add texture and tools to help you model your creations.

Create Textures

Old-fashioned metal combs can be great for scoring lines and creating texture. Saw blades can be helpful, as can an old garlic press for creating different texture effects. Use your imagination – Try taking some lace, for example, and pressing it into the clay to get a pretty pattern. Cookie cutters etc. can be drawn into service.

Creating Slabs

When making a nice small slab, a good old rolling pin will do just fine. However, if you need something a little bigger, find yourself a nice length of the curtain rod. Do be creative here as well – carve a design into an old rolling pin or wrap the rolling pin with different materials to see what textures you can create this way.

Cutting Wires

It is simple enough to make your own cutting wires. All you need is some fishing line and a couple of handles to tie it to. Curtain rings, large buttons or toggles can all do nicely.

Old Tools

There are a number of different tools that can be put to use to help you model the clay. Look out at thrift stores or flea markets to see if you can find tools that are suitable.

Old Credit or Gift Cards

These can be used as scrapers or to score lines or even cut into the specific shape that you want to use.

Get Creative

The main thing is to try and be a bit more creative – perhaps you have rubber stamps that you can use to create an impression, what about a textured button? Look around at the things you have at home before simply assuming that you will not be able to find anything else to use.

Kilns and Wheels

If you are just starting out, it is better to try your skills with a clay that you can bake in the oven. Kilns and potters' wheels can be expensive so it is important to ensure that this is something that you will get a lot of use out of before buying them.

I advise starting out using a polymer clay that can be set in the oven or an air-dry clay initially so that you can see if you really do want to continue. You can, if you like, build your own fire kiln so do research on Google and see if that is an option for you.

If you want to progress to clay that must be fired, try and see whether or not there are potters in the area that may agree to let you fire your pieces. Alternatively, seek out a course so that you get the feel for working with a wheel and kiln.

Buying a Pottery Wheel

This is a very expensive piece of equipment and should be reserved for when you are absolutely certain that this is something that you will carry on with. Start by looking at second-hand machines – you can find some at reasonable rates and in pretty good condition.

If you are planning on this as a business, an electric wheel should be seriously considered – the results are more consistent than what you would get with a manually operated wheel and it is a lot easier, and less tiring, to operate when compared to a manual machine. If you have a problem with co-ordination, do not even consider getting a manually operated wheel.

Buying a Kiln

As mentioned above, reserve this purchase for when you are certain that this is something that you will stick to over time. Ask yourself the following questions before looking for a kiln:

• How much space do I have? That big old kiln might seem like a good idea but do you have space for it?

How will I access the kiln or how will I transport it? The bigger the kiln, the harder it is to move. You need to know how to access the kiln so that you know whether to buy a top-opening kiln or a front-loader.

• How is my power supply? Kilns, even the smaller ones, require a good deal of power to operate. Make sure that your power supply can handle the type of kiln that you want to get.

- What quantities am I looking at making? If you will be making a lot, a bigger kiln makes sense. In general, though, your kiln should always be full when firing is done so that you can make the most out of it. It might pay to have a main kiln and a smaller one so that you can do some smaller orders as well.

- Will I be working in the same room as the kiln? This is not advisable because of the heat generated. If you have no alternative, you should consider firing items overnight instead.

- Can the floor and walls handle it? A kiln can be very heavy and it does give off a lot of heat. Do be sure that your floor and the walls around the kiln are able to withstand this heat. If possible, leave a space of at least a foot between the kiln and the walls.

Electrical kilns take a lot of the guesswork out of the process – you can set them for specific time periods and let them do their thing. Wood-burning kilns are praised by many purists but they are a lot of hard work – you need to keep feeding the fire while the items are being fired. Gas kilns can be a useful alternative.

You will also need to decide whether or not you want a front-loading kiln or a top-loading kiln. A front-loading kiln is generally a lot heavier and can be difficult to install but it will last a lot longer than a top-loading kiln. Top-loading kilns come in a range of sizes and can be more cost-effective to buy. You would have to choose which option fits better for you.

When it came to the pottery wheel, I advised you to buy a second-hand one. For a kiln, try to buy a new one, instead of a second-hand one if you can manage it. The reason is simple, progresses made in technology. The kilns of yesteryear were big, bulky and very inefficient when it came to energy usage. Do shop around a bit, though, you might get lucky and find a relatively new second-hand kiln.

Preparing the Clay

There is nothing more important when it comes to getting the outcomes that you are looking for than to prepare the clay properly.

Clay Preparation

You should always knead your clay before you start working with to ensure that it is malleable. Kneading ensures that the water within the clay is properly redistributed. It is better to knead only as much as you need for what you will be working with for that day.

Spiral Kneading

Form the clay into a rounded ball shape and then put your hands on either side. With your right hand, start pushing the clay down whilst, at the same time using your left hand to roll the clay. Rotate slightly after each pull. To check if you are getting the technique right, cut a cross-section through the clay – you should see it starting to form a spiral.

Ox-Head Kneading

Again, form the clay into a rounded ball and put your hands on either side. This time, imagine that you are trying to create horns for the clay. Push both sides simultaneously away from you. Reposition your hands and move all along the clay. Carry on until completely combined.

Reclaiming Old Clay

As a material for artists, clay is wonderful – even if it completely dries out, you can always reprocess it and you can do the same for scraps. As a result, there is no waste. The process is not a fun one but it is a good way to use up all the scraps, bits, and pieces.

Let the clay dry out altogether and cut it up into smaller bits. Put everything into a plastic container and add enough water to completely submerge the clay. It must soak overnight. The next day, get rid of any excess water and mix the clay well. Place in a thick layer on a plaster slab and leave to dry. Turn a few times in the process. When it is at a workable consistency, remove it and wedge it.

Wedging is necessary to get rid of any air bubbles – these can cause disastrous results during the firing process. Stack each of the sheets of clay and then beat until they become a solid brick. Cut the block in half lengthwise and then throw the one-half onto the other with force. Once again, beat until you have gotten a brick shape. Carry on in this manner until all the clay is mixed together.

Firing the Clay

Most clays need to be subjected to high heat conditions in order to properly set and strengthen them. There are some specialty clays that you can get that you are able to leave to air-dry or you can look out for Polymer clay which can be baked in the oven rather than in a kiln. The problem with these specialist clays is that they can end up becoming quite expensive overall and so may not be the best bet for your project and so we are going to stick to oven-baked clays.

If you do not want to go to the expense of buying a kiln because this is going to be more of a hobby than anything else, you can try building your own kiln. Do a Google search and you will find lots of advice about building your own kiln.

If you do decide that this is something that you can make a business out of, it does make sense to get a good quality kiln – when choosing one, consider the size of the items that you will be making, and how many you will be making.

Firing Your Clay

Generally speaking, you will fire the clay in two different stages – the first, or "biscuit" stage during which the clay undergoes a chemical transformation – it will still be porous but the hardness is now permanent. Once this stage is done, the items are easier to handle.

The second stage or "gloss" stage is where a glaze is bonded onto the surface of the item and it is usually used for decorative effect.

The Basic Technique for the "Biscuit" Phase

Remove the bungs from the kiln – you will replace them when the all the water has been driven off. Start off slowly with increases in temperature being no more 210F-300F per hour until you get to 930F. Hold something over the bung hole to ensure that there is no longer any steam coming out of it. If steam does still come out, wait until the temperature has gone up by another 50F and check again. (Do wear protective gloves as any steam that comes out will be hot.)

Once the water is gone, it is possible to increase the temperature faster. Most potters aim for a range of between 1760F-1830F ideal for this stage.

With this firing, you want to maximize your space as much as possible – you can stack pots rim to rim, as long as the top one is lighter or even place small objects inside upturned bowls. It is not a problem, at this stage, if the items do touch. You do, however, need to consider that some of the items will shrink so keep that in mind when packing the kiln.

It is important to note that the work should be completely dry before you begin to fire it.

The Basic Technique for the "Gloss" Phase

The most common method for firing a glaze is through oxidation. It is the easiest method to use and so it is advisable that beginners master this technique before moving on to others. It is the most predictable way to get the colors you are looking for.

As you progress, do look into Reduction firing techniques as well – just be sure that you research the process thoroughly first, or if possible, take a couple of classes because this can be pretty technical. With reduction firing, there is too much carbon monoxide in the kiln and the oxygen molecules in the clay and glaze are then taken up by the carbon monoxide and the chemical structure and color of the glaze changes as well.

Trouble-Shooting

Sometimes, even if you have prepared the shelves of the kiln as instructed by the manufacturer, they can bond to it. A good way to prevent this is to get some silica sand and place it on the shelf in a thin, even layer. This allows for some movement of the clay as it shrinks and dries.

Do be careful, however, to leave a space of about an inch all around the edges of the shelf so that none of the sand is pushed onto the work below.

You might also find that your pots are cracking or warping too much. If this is the case, it could be because of one of the following:

• The walls of the pot are not even and this has caused the distortion. If one wall is thicker than the other, for example, it can cause cracks or warping. The actual thickness of the clay you are working with is not important as long as all sides are even.

• Clay memory can cause distortions. This is most likely to occur when the clay was originally prepared for use – the clay retains its memory and will revert to its original shape when fired.

• The higher the level of plasticity in the clay, the higher the probability that it will warp. Counteract this tendency with the addition of grog or sand.

High-Temperature Clays

When working at higher temperatures, the rules change a bit. For gloss or glaze firing, you increase the temperature by 212F every hour until it gets to 842F and then turn it to its highest setting when setting your glazes.

Higher temperatures provide their own set of problems so you need to take extra care of the following:

• Make sure that there is no glaze at all on the feet or base of your bowl. If any drips onto the kiln shelf, the item will stick to the shelf.

• You need to make sure that the item is properly supported as well – do not use stilts in this case or you may end up with the clay slumping over.

• When firing at such high temperatures, you need to ensure that none of the bowls are touching the others or they will stick together.

Once the items have been fired, switch the kiln off and leave to cool before taking the pottery out.

Basic Techniques for Modeling Clay

This section, if we went into full details, could fill a few books on the subject so here we are just going to go through the basic techniques that you will find most useful. Master these techniques and then do some research and find others to improve your skills even further.

Slabbing

With this technique, you make your items from sheets of clay, rather than sculpting it from rolled clay. The key here is to ensure that the slabs are uniform in shape and thickness. You can do this by getting yourself a clay harp – the "harp" has notches evenly spaced along each side and you simply cut the slab by drawing the wire over your clay brick horizontally. You then drop the wire a notch and cut the next slab and repeat until you have enough slabs.

The clay harp can be on the expensive side to you can consider making your own simplified version by using pieces of wood in different thicknesses. Lay the clay in between the thickest set of wood pieces and drag your wire along the wood to cut the first slab. Swap the wood for one that is a little thinner and continue in this manner until you have the slabs that you need.

To ensure that each slab is the right thickness for your needs, cut two strips of wood to that thickness and place on either side of the slab. Rest the rolling pin on either side of these strips and roll the clay out with confidence – the wooden strips will prevent you from making your slab too thin.

You can join slabs together if you like simply by melding the two edges. Press them into one another so that the stick together, turn over and repeat.

Once you have the requisite number of slabs, you can form your shapes, decorate them or texturize them as required.

Pinching

Pinching is one of the basic lessons you learn when first starting out. It involves you getting stuck into the clay and getting your hands dirty. By actually being able to manipulate the clay with your hands, you get a better feel for how to manipulate it.

When starting out, add grog to the clay so that it is stronger. This allows you to practice your technique and leaves less chance of the clay cracking when fired.

Do always make sure that your hands are as cool as possible when working with clay so that it does dry out faster.

This is not a technique for someone who has long nails – keep your nails neatly trimmed or don't give this method a go at all.

Start out with prepared clay that has been rolled into a ball. It should fit snugly into the palm of your hand. Using the thumb of your other hand, press into the center of the ball until you can start to feel a bit of pressure on the palm of your hand. You want it no more than half an inch thick at the bottom – this will form the base.

Use your finger and thumb to pinch out the shape from the bottom of the ball. Rotate the clay after each little pinch and work your way in this manner until you have an established rhythm and the bowl shape starts to take shape. Continue until you have the shape that you require.

Always work upwards and outwards. If the pit becomes too floppy, use a hair dryer to dry the clay out a bit.

Making the Base

When you are satisfied with the size of the bowl, you can start working on making the base. Use your wooden spoon to gently smack the bottom of the bowl into a flat shape.

Smoothing it Off

When you are satisfied with the base, you can smooth off the outside and inside of the bowl using a kidney or metal scraper. If you like, draw a pattern on with a comb, knife, etc. or add little lumps or coils of clay to add interest before firing and glazing.

Coiling

This is one of the more traditional methods when it comes to working with clay and it is one of the simplest to learn. You would also be amazed at the kind of results that you can get, despite the simplicity of this method. This does require a little more patient, though – you roll out lengths of clay and then adhere them to form the shape that you want. You can then choose whether or not you want to further smooth out the end result.

Choosing the right clay here is extremely important when it comes to getting this technique right. You want a clay that is plastic enough not to crack when building up the coils. You also need to consider the end glazes that you are going to be applying and choose your clay color accordingly. Finally, consider how you are going to be firing the clay and choose a clay that will work well with that method.

Flat or Round Coils?

This depends on the project and the effect that you want to achieve. In both instances, you will roll the clay into a coil. When using round coils, you need to make sure that there is sufficient space for the coils to adhere to one another. Start with a diameter of around two inches and work with that. You can try smaller coils once you get the hang of the technique. Always roll the coils with the palms of your hands so that there are no finger marks on them.

When flattening a coil, you basically do the same thing, except that the diameter should be a little fatter. Flatten the coil as you go along, each time using the palm of your hand and not the fingers. It is best to put a silicone mat or piece of plastic on your work surface so that the clay does not stick to it. Every time you flatten a piece of the coil, lift the flattened end up so that it doesn't stay stuck to the work surface.

If you would like something a little more interesting than just a plain coil, you can always decorate the coils before forming your pot. Press into a mold to get a more textured look or stamp the surface. Even just pressing in the eraser end of a pencil at regular intervals can go a long way to creating a more beautiful pattern.

Guiding Yourself

When it comes to assembling the coils, how do you know that you are going to achieve the right shape in the end? You can give yourself a bit of help in the form of a template. Sketch out the basic shape that you are aiming to make onto thick card and cut it out. Your pot should fit into the negative area of the shape formed in this way. When making your template, do make sure that the base of it will sit at perfect right angles to the work surface or your risk making a pot that looks a little wonky.

Building Your Pot

From there, all that is needed is to lay the coils. Lay the second coil on top of the first and blend the two by pressing gently downwards towards the first coil. Carry on adding the coils until you have the shape that you want.

Finish off by using a paddle or scraper to smooth out the sides and remove finger marks, if required and decorate as you please.

Mixing the Techniques

When you have gotten the hang of things, there is nothing stopping you from combining techniques so that can get better effects. For example, you could start the bowl off using the pinched technique and finish it up with coils, this time leaving the coil shapes in place as a design element.

Throwing

I have left this until last because it is one of the most difficult techniques. I do suggest considering going to at least one class so that you can be sure that your technique is right. The big advantage of throwing is that it goes quite a bit faster than any of the other techniques and, once you get it right, you will find that the results are generally uniformly good each time.

Again the clay you use will be the deciding factor in the successful outcome of the project. You do need a clay that has good plasticity. Again, you also need to consider what you are making and the firing method you are using before coming to the final decision.

Smooth clay is needed for items that have a more delicate nature; Medium clay is best suited to items of tableware, pots, and ovenware. Coarse clay is necessary for pots that need to withstand a lot of stress – like those for outside or those that undergo high heat techniques.

Start off with a smooth or medium clay when beginning as these are easier to throw.

Preparing the Clay

The consistency of the clay here is more important than with any other technique so be prepared to do more kneading and wedging here. It may be tempting to start off with a softer clay but this won't hold up to the wheel as well so don't try to take shortcuts. Using clay that is too hard is also problematic on the wheel because you have to use a lot more pressure in order to build the walls. Once you have prepared your clay, break it up into as many pieces necessary, roll each piece into a ball and wrap in plastic until you are ready to use it.

Preparing to Throw the Clay

Get all the tools and items that you are going to use together ahead of time and keep them where you can get to them easily. When throwing, you do not have time to hunt around for a scraper, etc.

Throwing the Clay

Wipe the wheel with a damp sponge so that it is slightly damp and so that there are no traces of clay left on it. Take your ball of clay and place it as close to the center as you can – the secret to the success of this technique is to get the clay properly centered. Start the wheel up and center the clay. This is done by applying pressure to the top with one hand and to the sides with the other. Do not take too long with this or you risk overworking your clay. You may need to add more water as you go along – your hand needs to glide over the clay easily.

You should wear some sort of protective apron and old clothes for this – it is messy. There are some people that worry about the clay dust but I honestly do not think that it is really that much of an issue. I have a couple of pairs of jeans and old t-shirts for wearing when I throw pottery and I usually try to remember to put on an apron as well.

Opening up the Clay

Now the fun really starts – you are going to start forming your item. Using your right thumb, keeping it flat, find the center of your clay and press down on it. Push down so that you start to see a donut shape forming. You must keep your thumb flat.

Make a Good Base

The base of your pot needs to be strong so be sure to compress the clay by running your thumb over the center and out to the outside edge three times. When complete, pull your thumb up against the wall and start to shape your pot.

Shaping your Pot

There are a lot of hand positions that you can adopt but here are the three most important ones:

Using your thumb and forefinger, gently pinch the clay and lift at the same time, a little at a time.

When the wall has started to form, place your right hand on the outside of the clay and continue pinching and raising the wall. What you want is a tapering effect so that the base is wider. After each lift, gently hold the rim between the fingers of your left hand and apply pressure with the fingers of your right hand. Carry on lifting, pinching and smoothing in this manner. If the rim becomes too uneven, slow the wheel right down and cut it off with a knife or potter's wire.

Once you are satisfied that the pot is taking shape nicely, it is time to knuckle up. Wrap your forefinger around your thumb and form a fist with the same hand. Place the fingers of your other hand inside the pot, allowing the thumb to rest on the top of the fist that you made. Apply slight pressure and lift the pot as many times as necessary until you get the size that you want. When you have the height, relax the pressure and allow the top to come back to a round shape again. If you take away your hands too quickly, the form is likely to wobble.

Lifting Off the Wheel

Take off any excess clay at the base of the pot by holding a rib at a 45-degree angle to the pot. Then make a bevel at the base of the pot so that you can pass the wire through easily. Get rid of any clay bits lying on the wheel and pass the wire under the base of the pot. Make sure that your hands are dry and grasp the pot near the base gently. Start to lift away from you and place on a board as quickly as possible.

Decorative Techniques

Decorating the final product is most of the fun. You could use a glaze and color or mark a pattern into the sides – depending on the look that you are trying to achieve.

Decorating on the Wheel

Once you have your basic cylinder shape, there is a lot that you can do to decorate it on the wheel.

Change the Shape

Tired of making round cylinders? Then why not do a square one? After you have thrown the pot, switch off the wheel and simply pull your fingers up the inside of the pot to form a rough square. When you have the basic shape right, use a dowel to define each corner.

Using a Cylinder Stamp or Cog

Slow the wheel down a lot and bring the cog/ stamp up against the outside where you want the pattern to be and support the inside with your hand.

Too Groovy

Take a comb and slow the wheel right down. With your hand supporting the inside of the pot, apply the comb gently to the surface so that it carves out grooves. What I like to do is to use a cheap plastic comb – I break off a few of the teeth so that the pattern has patches of smooth surfaces every few rows of grooved surfaces.

An old credit card can also be cut so that you can create a pattern on the outside of your pot in a similar manner.

If fine, well-defined grooves do not appeal to you, you can use your finger to form the ridges instead.

Decorating off the Wheel

There are so many ways that you can make patterns on your finished project – basically, anything that makes a mark on the outside of the pot will allow you to decorate the pot. Try using rubber stamps, pencils, lace, anything you can think of.

Techniques for When the Pots Are Nearly Dry

With these techniques, you need to strike a balance between firm enough to handle and still pliable enough that the pot does not crack when manipulated. It can take a bit of practice to get this right at first but once you do, you are going to have a lot of fun decorating.

Indenting

Place the fingers of one hand on the inside of the pot and the fingers of the other on the outside. Gently press in the wall so that you make an indentation, whilst supporting the wall with your other hand. Repeat until you have the desired pattern, alternating hands – push in one spot to the inside of the pot and push the next out to the outside to create a pattern of indentations and bulges.

Alternatively, you can just choose a pattern of indentations or a pattern of bulges.

Squaring the Pot

Lay the pot on its side so that it flattens a little. Repeat on each side until the pot is square in shape. Tap gently so that the edges are better defined.

Faceting

If you plan to use this method, you need to ensure that the pot wall was initially thicker than normal. Use a potato peeler to shave out facets, starting at the base and tapering upwards. The potato peeler should not be used in the kitchen again later.

Fluting

Again, this requires the pot wall to be a bit thicker. You use a loop tool to carve out grooves along the outside of the pot. These can be horizontal or vertical, depending on what you want to achieve. Choose a random pattern or a repeating one, as you like.

Decorating with Slip

There are no hard and fast rules when it comes to decorating with slip – basically liquid clay – but it is amazing how many different effects you can achieve.

Use the slip as is or color it with a stain and then decorate the item with it. You can choose to dip the whole item in the slip to get an even color – just make sure that it is as dry as leather and that you dip it quickly so that it doesn't get too saturated.

If the item is difficult to lift, you can pour the slip over the outside of it.

Alternatively, apply with a paint brush and create whatever pattern you like – do let it dry a bit before applying the second coat, though.

A lot of the techniques that artists use with paint can be adopted here. Sponge the slip on, or apply it using rags to get different textures.

You can also spatter the slip onto the item using an old toothbrush.

You do not have to stop when the slip is on, though – you can scratch a pattern out of the slip so that the pottery underneath shows through as well. (This needs to be done while the slip is still wet.)

You can also make use of stencils and slip to decorate the surface of the item – tape the stencil down sponge or brush on the slip. Allow it to dry and remove stencil.

Slip Trailing

This involves pouring the slip on using the fine nozzle. Do practice a bit first because this is a difficult technique to master. Here is where you need the medicine dropper or fine-nozzled bottle.

Feathering

This is really only good for flat surfaces because the slip needs to be pretty liquid. What I do like about this technique is that it is easier to hide mistakes. Start by covering the surface in slip and then draw equidistant, horizontal lines across this, while it is still wet, in a different color. Using a fine tipped needle, draw vertical lines in the slip that you have poured so that you get a feathered effect.

Marbling

Very similar to the above technique, except that here you pour the two colors in and gently swirl them. You can also run a needle through to get a more marbled look. Be careful not to overdo it, though – if you mix them too much they will combine and all contrast will be lost.

Wax Resist

With this technique, you apply hot wax to areas that you do not want the slip to adhere to. The wax repels the slip for an interesting effect.

Burnishing

If you want your pots to be really shiny, then this may be the effect for you. When the item is leather-hard, rub it with the back of a spoon until a shine develops. Finish off by wiping it with a clean cotton ball. Do be careful not to get fingerprints on the outside and use a low temperature firing technique. Anything over 1832F will destroy the finish.

Incising

This will also take a little bit of practice but can be so effective. Cut away sections of the item when it is at the leather-hard stage to create a pattern. You can, if you like, draw the pattern on first so that you have a guide to work from. Do use a sharp knife and cut slowly and carefully. Do be careful that you are not completely destroying the structural integrity of the finished piece but do have fun with this technique. Nervous about cutting out a pattern? Why not change the shape of the rim?

Glazes

Glazes are commonly used to add a different finish or color to clay. The clay should be fired first and allowed to cool before the glaze is applied. The finished item is then fired again to set the glaze.

Glazes come in a range of colors, materials and textures, depending on what you want to achieve. Do check that the glaze you want to use will work well with the clay you are using and the firing technique you want to employ.

Glazes do open up a whole new range of options when it comes to either enhancing your item or changing the look of it altogether. It is important to do a bit of research on how each glaze will react as some will change color depending on the firing method used.

Glazes can be applied in much the same ways as I listed for slip, the difference being that they should be applied after the first firing, not while the item is still drying.

Conclusion

Thank you for downloading this book.

I do hope that you have been bitten by the pottery bug and are dying to start your first project. I hope that you have fun with it and enjoy learning how to master the basics.

Once you have got the basics down, I urge you to explore, to try new things, to always be on the lookout for new projects. I urge you to try out your own ideas and to use this book as a reference point for your future research.

What I love about working with clay is that there are so many techniques to explore. Mistakes can be made but the materials can be reused so I feel free to explore, knowing that nothing really does go to waste with this technique.

All that is left now is for you to get out there and to get started. Have fun with this and remember that your clay wants to be molded into form – give it a new voice and express yourself at the same time!

Win a free

kindle
OASIS

Let us know what you thought of this book to enter the sweepstake at:

http://booksfor.review/clay

Printed in Great Britain
by Amazon